THE PORTAGE POETRY
SERIES

Series Titles

The Found Object Imagines a Life: New and Selected Poems
Mary Catherine Harper

Naming the Ghost
Emily Hockaday

Mourning
Dokubo Melford Goodhead

Messengers of the Gods: New and Selected Poems
Kathryn Gahl

After the 8-Ball
Colleen Alles

Careful Cartography
Devon Bohm

Broken On the Wheel
Barbara Costas-Biggs

Sparks and Disperses
Cathleen Cohen

Holding My Selves Together: New and Selected Poems
Margaret Rozga

Lost and Found Departments
Heather Dubrow

Marginal Notes
Alfonso Brezmes

The Almost-Children
Cassondra Windwalker

Meditations of a Beast
Kristine Ong Muslim

Mary Catherine Harper's *The Found Object Imagines a Life* is a journey well worth taking. The art of her New and Selected Poems is not removed from the Earth, it seems akin to gravity itself. Necessary. Ardent. Constant. The urgency of expression bridges matter and light with living flesh and love's lasting hunger. Throughout this fine collection, she explores the labyrinth of ambiguity between memory and the moment, between abstraction and the tangible. Her poems guide the reader along high lines of mountains to fragile views of mortality. Harper's voice is authentic, perceptive, and sensitive. Like a rock climber, her poems are juxtaposed between the ethereal and the empirical. Yet Mary Catherine Harper does not fear the fall into human imperfection, her flight is real, her "own heart pumping / against the end of the world."

—**Mark B. Hamilton**
author of *OYO, The Beautiful River*

Mary Catherine Harper's *The Found Object Imagines a Life* is at once earth-grounded and wonder-laced. Here, "words that buzz loose in the mouth / are given over to the clay that made the world." Traveling from Midwestern farm roots to rock climbs, through domesticity and desire, Harper's poems employ both archetype and direct revelation. The resulting collection is polyvocal yet intimate, as at home in the story of Persephone as when addressing the "sycamore in my ex-lover's side yard" or untangling threads of family history. There is pain here, yes, but I was struck most by the lushness of the world seen through Harper's language. How can't we fall in awe, again, at the "ruby gleam" of beets, the "cloud-to-cloud lightning," the "tattoos slithering up" a friend's arms? This is a collection alive to the world and rich with what it finds there.

—**Laura Donnelly**
author of *Midwest Gothic*

Mary Catherine Harper takes us on an intellectual romp through culture, mythology, and religion. Whether she is "Spelunking with Persephone" (that "trippy" girl), conversing with the snake from The Garden of Eden ("Did you even try to pick me up? I'm not slimy at all . . ."), or discussing the creation of the universe with Grandmother Spider, you trust her knowledge and admire her talent. In poems both challenging and playful, she knows how facts can become revelations ("Blue Crow Eyes"), understands that Apocalypse is earned, and that consciousness can be snatched by a dragonfly, a moth, an earwig. . . . Or maybe even a poet.

—**Cathryn Essinger**
author of *The Apricot and the Moon*

The work of Mary Catherine Harper has an intimacy of speech that makes me believe every word as if confided via a truth serum. Yet those very words also remind me that every story is "conspiring with its / artist against veracity." In her most recent collection, Harper investigates the complex relationship between story and truth on deeper and deeper levels: from our personal family histories to our cultural mythologies; from the animal story of our bodily world to the mental world exercising poetic examination itself. Using imagery as intricate as blown-egg art and language as delicious as Persephone's pomegranate, *The Found Object Imagines a Life* invites us to explore storytelling's contradictions viscerally by "unzippering our skins to enter the story." Inside, readers will discover that the fine line between truth and lying—which the author humbly calls misremembering—is actually masterful creation.

—**Amy Wray Irish**
author of *Breathing Fire* and *The Nature of the Mother*

The Found Object Imagines a Life

New and Selected Poems

Mary Catherine Harper

Cornerstone Press
Stevens Point, Wisconsin

Cornerstone Press, Stevens Point, Wisconsin 54481
Copyright © 2022 Mary Catherine Harper
www.uwsp.edu/cornerstone

Printed in the United States of America by
Point Print and Design Studio, Stevens Point, Wisconsin 54481

Library of Congress Control Number: 2022938212
ISBN: 979-8-9861447-1-9

Epigraph from "To an Aged Bear," from *The Death of Sitting Bear* by N. Scott
Momaday. Copyright © 2020 by N. Scott Momaday. Used by permission of
HarperCollins Publishers.

Cornerstone Press titles are produced in courses and internships offered by the
Department of English at the University of Wisconsin–Stevens Point.

DIRECTOR & PUBLISHER   EXECUTIVE EDITOR
Dr. Ross K. Tangedal   Jeff Snowbarger

SENIOR EDITORS
Lexie Neeley, Monica Swinick, Kala Buttke

PRESS STAFF
Rhiley Block, Alyssa Bronk, Grace Dahl, Patrick Fogarty, Ava Freeman, Angela
Green, Brett Hill, Cale Jacoby, Hunter Keisow, Adam King, Jeremy Kremser, Amanda
Leibham, Leo McEvilly, Abbi Wasielewski, Abbi Rohde

In memory of Barbara,
who taught me to honor
the stories of shadows.

Poems

Stories to Misremember

Spelunking for Persephone

Surprising the God of Motion

Earning Apocalypse

The Untamed Grave of Us

The Found Object Imagines a Life

Mortality is your shadow and your shade....
Keep to the trees and waters. Be the singing of the soil.
—N. Scott Momaday, "To an Aged Bear"

Stories to Misremember

The Lifecycle of a Memory

This shadow, this creature, this dogged thing
memory
as hollow as an egg with its insides blown out
and painted painstakingly with a scene
that never quite matches how it feels to be
real

Think of a carton of empty shells, each telling
facts
as true to form as humanly possible, given
the art imposed by a curved miniature
surface

Think of precisely rendered scenes never quite
true
to the weight of a birth or holiday or mating
ritual, to the heft of aging or solitude in death,
to the surprise of first learning the world is not
flat

Think of pigment glistening on the lopsided
sphere
a viscous doppelganger conspiring with its
artist against veracity, yet desperate to be glued
together

What Shoes Do

I hated my mother
as all good girls do
sometimes
because there were too many
pairs of unused shoes
in her closet, hoarded there,
a heart beating only for itself.

But how could love be measured
by the amount of dust falling
on thirteen pairs of red shoes,
I chided myself.

I loved my mother
most of the time
remembering we both worry over
what weather the day might bring,
this as all farm women
in my family are apt to do.

And apt to stare into the mirror
where my skin has taken on the
texture of dried leather,
like that single pair of shoes
left in the garden
untended, splitting open.

And apt to exaggerate
the count of shoes
and the texture of memory,
gaps where the past should be,
that oblique place
I cannot quite describe
except to say it was small,
cramped with the clutter
of at least a hundred high heels
and no clear faces.

Survivor's Story

I don't know any of you
others before me who stumbled from the old world
after your forced conversion,
after the ruin of your army-trampled crops,
after the potato blight wasted our family,

only the rattle of a new-world diamondback
just before being hacked into pieces in a garden
weeded up with thorns and devil's horns,
a sticker patch my mother could never eradicate.

My story hasn't the ferocity
of a hounding law and futile attempts to escape it,
no scenes of momentary relief for hungry lips,
no rags of clothing distributed to worn-thin bodies
dragging around their equally tired souls.

My story pales,
nevertheless here she is, my mother
heavy with survivor's guilt, yes, arriving at the end
of blight and rape, and prayer that could get you killed,

yes, but a woman strong-willed as venom
with enough bite to her
to never beg for food her several hungers long,
to never willingly bare her nether parts—let alone

her soul—to anyone at any time
ever again,
here baring fangs as long-reaching as a garden hoe
when the rattlesnake coils, aiming for me.

Feuding Clans

Violence begets violence begets
violence, until the thick saturation
of it blooms out of its borders,
an unexpected moment—call it
blessing, call it grace, call it
love—where all the trauma
cradled down in the gut
of generations is thrown away
as naturally as children wandering
into the demilitarized zone
between innocence and experience.

Children throw their hearts
across the border and into
the fray, fearless, headlong,
trusting—even as they swallow
the horror of it—that every
terrible detail of the story
will be written out loud,
then thrown away forever.

Breath Between Two Souls

People drive through fences
sometimes for no good cause
simply because they must,
a scalp crawling with an itch
so intense that it drives a body
into a ditch, off an overpass.

If bodies fall long enough,
for example out of a plane
or off the South Rim's edge,
they have ample time to settle
into the motion, to separate
from the metaphysics of it,
to forget the jump's purpose
and notice the leg's weight,
the functionality of the hand
as thumb and fingers spread.

What we once called destiny
is now a double-helix ladder
that if unwound would span
the breath between two souls,
bringing them almost close
enough for one to touch the
other's hair with fingertips
just before the bones break
together at the bottom of
the fall, marrow melding.

This self-exposing story
wastes despair, except for
what I face in the plummet,
the same coarse hair texture
the same high cheekbones
the same desperate hands
unfisting, stretching across.

Eclipse of the Past

Version 1

I was born to the planet of now.
I've witnessed a full eclipse of the past.
My mother tells me that as a baby
I laughed at nothing in particular,
that by the age of five I declared
knowledge of everything just told me
because any telling is mere reiteration.

Version 2

I was born to the motherless world.
I learned to sleep lightly in the dead
of winter, for my dreams were apt
to smother me with the weight
of my father's body. Decades later
I'm still his child, small-boned and
easily held under by feather pillows.

Version 3

I was born to the story of the lost.
I became the keeper of memories,
recalling my mother's baby face
as she sat in the lap of a stranger.
My ears still ring from the clock
striking three above her head. If only
details could screw down the past.

Version 4

I was born to the warden of time.
I still sometimes crack myself
into tiny pieces, like the crayons
I used to snap in half and secret in
my grandmother's three-cornered
kitchen as I chanted spells. Narrow
rooms sometimes need magic.

Dreaming in Wichita, Early November

This room of dreaming
my father fully alive and walking in rhythm,
one step per second, he'd say,
rumbling his voice around a song or waltzing
my mother through the rooms
he grew his children in,
wrapping us in layers of wool blankets,
humming to hold chest cavities
together in winter,
untrussing us from tightly packed rooms
every time the vernal equinox called.

That was then, this is now
a hospital room,
a pace of twelve steps,
turning for twelve more,
turning in this
cube of a dozen feet.

Now something shifts
on the bed to the everywhere
of what will prove to be my last dream of him
tramping through
miles of high-ceilinged rooms
of pastureland and sky-blue walls,
a staircase rising
beside a sequoia-topping tree
breezing beneath light originating
from incandescent bulbs so high above him
they seem the size of pinpricked night,
their sparkle the promise of an ever-larger room,
his ever-expanding chest
humming free and bodiless.

That was then, this is now
my lungs suddenly emptied of song,
rhythm flattened in this
cube of a dozen feet.

8

Sonic Booms

Some families attach name tags
to every conversation,
every pause in conversation,
every tone shift,
every hand gesture,
as if naming could make it
easier to control each other's
sound from the outside in.

Some families expel verbs
and clusters of verbs,
omitting as many as possible
because verbs cause so much
touch among the world's objects,
because verbs require so much
breath to blow them over.

Some families are by nature,
by breeding or both, enervated
by the whisper that bodies make
tiptoeing through rooms,
as if any elliptical paths crossing
would result in collision, as if
any touch would produce sonic booms.

Sandpaper in the Toolbox

One of my daughters declares
it's just the human condition,
the puzzling dysfunction
of a family meant to cocoon
us through birth and baptism,
through anniversary and death.

This vortex of urgent calls
packing us together in the small
space of the old farmhouse,
ostensibly for warmth and
company when a blizzard
takes out the power lines.

Every family storm blows us
back to the gritty sensitivities
we thought we'd bound tight
in layers of bubble wrap
and secreted in the drawers
and closets of our childhood.

Unexpectedly exposed and raw,
we are baffled up by that sharp
urge to rub each other the wrong
way once again, forgetting
our vow of maturity, failing
to leave the coarse-grit sandpaper

in the toolbox where it belongs.
We, the aging six of a sensible
carpenter, still compelled
to hammer out complaints,
wasting our good company,
waiting for power to be restored.

Pulling Wings Off Onions

This intense focus on full disclosure—threshing the wheat
soundly to discard the chaff, then separating bran from core,
the graham scattered dry upon my palm—only leaves
my hands chapped, in need of therapeutic lotion.

I have worked this rough honesty so long that I find
pulling wings off onions has left me with irritated eyes
and a dull mind, this desire to expose the body's necessary
rules—like Lear in his final act, exhausted after carrying
the dead body of love onto the stage—reducing me
to the urge to just let go, that easy act of blaming
the world for growing faulty humans, layer upon layer,
that easy act of forgiving my own part in the drama.

I know any such quit-claim is impossible, that even as
the generations of me continue to jumble and tumble down,
I am like the old concrete wall crumbling beside the family
barn, the color of the wall mirroring the blood-red paint I stir.

Recording that thought in this brief soliloquy is neither gift
nor curse, only a fleeting truth in an overexposed drama
paced to the slow-dry of onion layers, paced to the imagined
wings of a cicada buzzing above as I finger a discarded shell.

Blue Spruce

They were freaks,
odd conical shapes
bordering on slate blue
not the color of real trees
I told my father as he planted them.

Unwelcome bristles,
pain against the skin
nothing to snake my arms into
nothing like the garden elm
nothing fit to bear a tire swing.

But what an exhibition
that next spring,
that bloom of lime
tear drops wagging pure
green legitimacy.

Me fingering the velvet wonder
turning green with want
knowing which tree to love best
how to choose wisely
if I ever had the chance again.

Train Stories

I mimic my father's hospitality
to strangers, tell nostalgic stories
of long-ago farm life to fellow
passengers, cocoon-close
on a train bound for a place
made to scatter us.

The certainty of that future
endpoint, the conviction of what
the past should mean, even
the statically charged present,
given up to the liminality
of this incidental community.

Each story of what was never quite
true jostling us toward familiarity,
making the squeeze of space
the narrowness of time
the differences among strangers
inconsequential.

Train travel forces us to resize
our lives before disembarking,
we gather our possessions
stuff our rucksacks, know
we can't leave the heavy truth
of the past behind on warm seats.

Edging Away

I took these photos of an old elm tree—maybe even old
enough to be ancient, its trunk so massive—rooting
a town that edges off the continent.

It is reminding me of the two elms in our garden,
gifting me the near-lost memory of you on the rope
swing that dangled down from the sky—or so its origin
seemed—when we were children.

Our trees died of Dutch Elm disease, but not before
swinging our childhood away.

I can still—almost—feel the bite of the rough hemp noose
on the ball and sides of my feet, as I swung two stories
high, making an arc so wide and deep I could have been
the moon's half-full twin.

Let me frame this tree—including the dead leaves hanging
beside their green snaggletoothed siblings—to remind me
of our long-gone trees, but also because the outline of you
has started to fade.

Frostbitten Skin

If only it were not my brother
with all his weary dispossessions
stuffed in plastic grocery bags
in a booth too antiquated for good use.

What if it were I myself mumbling
to the sky, an exchange of bodies,
me missing those teeth my brother lost
while jumping from the cottonwood.

Listen. I swear I hear my own breath
over this underused phone line,
his jaw set and travelling light
without a high wire to stand on,

my face splattered with his sweat,
his blood escaping me
in rivulets down my fingers
too numb to feel the old receiver.

I need to slough off the thick
of his skin, try to believe
he didn't want to die, only see
that mythic wall of orange sky.

See. I swear when I press my fingers
against my eyelids, I see behind
these eyes a wall of orange fire,
a fire to light his unfinished story,

the decades of wind turbines that grew
between us falling away, leaving him
perched in the garden cottonwood,
his hands silver as the underside of leaves

reaching for me through sage-tinted air
and smelling like a juniper berry
rolled between thumb and finger
so tightly the pulse cracks the seed.

Look. I swear the color of a cottonwood
matters, needs to have never been
too bleached to bear fluff, needs to be
green if only to propagate frostbite.

I need him still rolling that juniper berry
in his mouth, still humming behind
what teeth he possessed
in the place beyond his childhood

always looking for a better tree,
the juniper grown too crowded for company,
the cottonwood too blighted white
to be trusted, but him still climbing.

Feel. I swear when I was a child
I thought silly putty was invented for me,
pliable, elastic, smooth to the touch,
unlike the mildewed hemp rope

he struggled around his waist
and used to drop from that limb
as if to close the distance between
a mere body and the everlasting cosmos.

I swear I see his arm become the rope,
his eyes the fire of the Pleiades,
my refusal to see the flash of a muzzle
aimed at the pulse of the planet.

I swear if he leaves me here
with my fingers pressing eyes shut
against a sun that bleaches cottonwoods
and eyelids to paper-white,

I swear if he spends his blood
in that grimy, broken phone booth
in a body already wasted
to the translucence of frostbitten skin

with only my own heart pumping
against the end of the world, I swear
I'll cut the rope around his waist
and inhale the bright orange air.

Stories to Misremember

There are events to be told
exactly as they happened,
bare facts, no euphemizing,
to be regurgitated, re-tasted
once, twice, but on the third
time to be misremembered.

This to be done intentionally,
to stare down the rattlesnake
just after it strikes the shin
before its acid melts the heart
before the eye burns to blink,
this a spell to deflect poison.

Truth be told, it is no miracle
to survive snakebite without
antivenin or amputation:
only get to the third telling
and send the story pulsing
toward misremembrance.

Heaven Spin Open

The day we buried his ashes
our brother's Karma found us,
bringing with it that funnel cloud
wide enough to swath through the house,
barn, outbuildings of the home that owns us.

Nature's test out of the southwest aimed straight
at the five of us standing in a row on the sidewalk,
that arm of sky kissing ground
as if to taunt us with the threat of embrace.

The alarm of a family craving family,
winding siblings tight for death
even as we entreat each other to scatter.

Our brother's stormy mind rotating
not low enough to lift the roof,
just close enough to prime a vacuum,
to empty our lungs of yearning.

And I swear it was then I saw heaven spin open
as if to say he loves us
like wind loving loose shingles just before
it sends the hail pelting down.

Planet of Chairs

The morning news reports a study,
somebody's findings of a direct correlation
between high crime rates and populations
having an above-average percentage of men,
the commentator finishing with a bold
caution against a world of men.

But what of a world of women,
where the generations of mothers suffer
anxiety through the unremitting rebellion
of clear-skinned daughters in slinky dresses,
and the generations of daughters endure
the open arms of the long-suffering?

It's not quite like utopian page turners
scribbled well over a century ago,
where the children of women wander
insouciantly, protected by watchful trees,
where the queen of the forest reclines
against an oak, nursing her young.

Instead the story of a planet of chairs
dusted daily but seldom warmed by
girl bones, mother spread, grandmother
ache, this the house that Jill keeps
for herself, armed with 39 bleached socks,
a loaf of bread, and a pair of pinking shears.

The Art of Love

How much easier to limn dead things,
every variation in skin tone,
the discolored fingernail,
the gunmetal gray hair of a corpse,

than sketch a living person,
an exercise in disproportion,
the living leg too long,
fattened waist too thick,
expressive face misshapen,
empty breast too slack,
uplifted arm a blur,
old body slumped,

fingers closed in on themselves
and weak with tremors,
useless for holding another's hand,

all the messy manners of living
complicating the artist's craft,
distractions from the art of love.

The Fall

Maybe a dance on an ice-polished surface
is a kind of truth,
not a denial but a glide across appearance,
an invitation to an honestly averted gaze.

I still have the skates that remember her feet,
still feel her heat,
still notice something about the last time
she ice skated,
she curving into me and saying something
about the cost of mothering,
something broken loose as I fell
from her body,
something about a ruined pelvis,
or was it something about what she saw
under the ice,
a body with frozen-open eyes,
flat and dull.

Maybe listening to strangers in a darkened room
is a good substitute,
the theft of someone else's life,
no need to interrogate an eye,
the sound of the story enough
to work its way in.

Like the story I write now to soften
the edges of the past,
the story of the squirrel I stopped to watch
just yesterday on my daily walk,
her body upright,
a perfect silhouette,

her tail curved against her head,
her one eye full of morning light,
seeing me
and remaining sideways
to take me in
with her vast peripheral view,
and me looking back at her
directly,
falling into her glassy black eye.

Leave the Casket Open

Once upon a time the universe
a noun,
a body thick and hot,
such muscle-knot energy bound
to erupt spasm
orgasm,
noun turned inside out,
this firestorm spiraling out
upon its own empty,
the simultaneous full
motion
of stars and weighted planets,
and so we juggernaut on
as far as we imagine forever
can take us.

When the skin is breached
what first verb to be
released
in the eruption,
the blood inflamed as oxygen
hits,
red splash rivering out
around yellow fat
clouding,
fibrous muscle coagulating,
intestine tumbling
onto its knees,
this to reverberate,
to be memorial to
the once-upon-a-pressure-cooking
body
that spiraled us all.

Leave the casket open to the air
convectioning,
the sentence mumbling "she looks
so natural
so alive,"
our story of origin just under
the leathered skin
ready to erupt.

Sgraffito

Hunger sits in the hollow of the upper back,
not in the stomach's pit, as our bodies misinform us.

Here, wing bones might yet issue from the scapula,
it only takes years of the right diet, thick with calcium,

and a friend with sandpaper, pressure-sensitive hands,
and the patience to scour layers of skin away

gently, to meet confined wings at the precise moment
they must unfold and shake feathers into air,

or be left forever hunched over the shoulder blades
like the curve of a gibbous moon, never quite full.

It is the scraping away that matters most, for in truth,
wings begin to pupate with the first slough of skin.

The hunger abates not from any steady diet but
once the body opens its breath of wings.

Now the true ordeal: hunger replaced by bafflement,
what to do with these appendages.

Thinning to Rag

I

Cold morning slapping me to life, a sharp blessing
of deep breaths, flexible muscle, dense bone
bearing my heavy heart as I step into your kitchen.

Ugly house an old comfort, bare wood, leaky roof
sagging backbone almost stopping the wind,
almost blocking the grit we used to pack between us.

Gone three months, yet suddenly here you are
pulling cookies from the oven, then just as sudden
your body gone, an evaporation into the death you are.

II

What more is there but to smell the Ponderosa Pine
scraping against your kitchen's half-open window,
its fragrance equal to the open bottle of vanilla extract.

What more is there but to find your cotton bedspread
long ago consigned to the bottom drawer of your chest,
the repository of items too worn even for your poverty.

What more but to spread it across your bed, to sleep
under it one two nights. Better yet, to be the profligate,
to take it home and use it, let it thin to a ghostly rag.

Beets

After staining my hands with their peelings,
after thin-slicing them, revealing their ruby gleam,
after dropping them in a pot of boiling water
along with islands of peppers, potatoes, carrots,
and cabbage, to be churned into a wine-stained sea,

after setting the table with my mother's chipped china
from the Dirty 30s, after stirring through the hour
it takes before I ladle soup into the bowls, dyeing
the red roses painted there an even darker shade
—almost too dark for my family's comfort,
dark as blood pudding—only then does she limp

across the threshold   between her grave
and my kitchen   in her white nurse's shoes,
as splattered with blood as when she last butchered
chickens six summers ago, only then does she
step in to dip her finger in the borscht and lick
with satisfaction, only then to red-lip her approval,

only then to wipe her stained hand on my apron,
to remind me that while this might not be
my favorite soup nor red my favorite color,
she's still my mother, and they're her favorites.
With that, I call my daughters to dinner.

Spelunking for Persephone

Diving In

I

How to stare at the rising sun
without burning the retina out

How to survive the tidal pull
without jeering at the moon

How to climb to the summit
without getting struck by lightning

How to walk the knife edge
without bleeding to death

How to spelunk to the earth's core
without running out of oxygen

How to unhinge heaven's door
without falling to Tartarus

II

Try practicing levitation above the water
to be planted in the sea breeze

You will feel the tug of the tide
but mostly the riptide

Dare to send your roots into the stone
that wombs all gods of the underworld

Find yourself resisting the urge
to interrogate your own contrary motions

Dig to the heart of mud while fastening
your eyes on the white of clouds

There is no diving in
without first swallowing the waterfall

Stone Veneer

We each attempt a poem about you
or if bold enough write directly to you,
we confused spelunkers of the heart
never getting it quite right
interchanging "you" and "us"
perhaps too enamored of Death
or still rebelling against Demeter
as if our mothers were the problem.

And yet we are sincere in the process
hoping our jabber will get you
to respond, even in your oblique way,
a vibration in the cave of us
the hollow between ribs
the place we are hoping
you'll visit some winter
instead of hibernating with your god.

If not, perhaps you would gift us
with the sound of bees gathering
or at least poke your finger through
the stone veneer of one of us.

Falling from a Cliff

Just before it happened
I was near the bottom watching
you near the top
after you had barked at me
to follow

My refusal shocked even me
my body fuming that you were taking
the usual route up
with me left to sniff your heels
to come in second
in such a common way

The impulse took me
and I broke the first rule
the absolute necessity to put aside
the end point and climb as if
positioning the fingers
at the end of my arm is the only
mechanics of being

as if each stretch
for a narrow ledge just above
marks the moment of creation

as if the leg and its foot lifted
to seek higher purchase
is the expansion of a universe

as if the muscles contracting
to pull the torso up
is the coagulation of a planet
with no end of it in mind

as if I am the spider
that by happenstance crawls
time and space and matter
into being

It should have been
just me and the rock face
I was hugging
into existence
but I climbed otherwise
with gritty speed
to compete with you before
you could reach the top

Just as I passed you
to my left

> *just as my fingers dug*
> *into the untested edge of the cliff*

> *just as my automatonic foot rose*
> *from the near-last toehold*

> *just before I could heave*
> *myself over the top*

the stone crumbled
to sand in my hand

Before the beginning and ending
of things in space could matter

> *before a body could land on its back*
> *precisely where it had started from*

> *before a head could crack open*
> *and its memory leak forth*

I became the freefall
to the other side of time

Persephone in Summer

She reveals that it was she who seduced him by plucking a narcissus
from her garden and mashing it between her thumb and forefinger
After anointing his eyelids and lips with the fragrant oil, she led him
to her pomegranate tree and enthralled him with the color of her heart

She tells me she returns to him because her wishbone was broken
not by him but in an accident of nature involving her mother.
Evidently, when a woman finds her daughter to be too much like her
the stars notice and make a correction to misalign one or the other body

Then she and I go at it, this during the heat of July and August when
as she puts it, she buzzes through the bulrushes looking for ripe bodies
to pollinate, ripe as the men and women oiled for tanning on the beach
I am too spellbound, too drugged up in her, to care about her purpose

Afterwards, she tells me she returns because she likes the sex with him
but only during what we air, tree, and ground dwellers call The Night
Generally, she finds him much too moody during the daylight hours
too narcissistic, she laughs, for any meaningful day-to-day activities

Later, she describes him as the most attentive god she's ever met
she returns each fall because he cries when she leaves, wastes away
He dotes on her all winter, wrapping her in textures of minerals
only found in the underworld, reminding her that she too is immortal

And thus our conversations go, me learning everything about her
or nothing, except that she is made of several stories, several voices
All these women, their faces like petals opening and closing in turn
charming me toward the cave's cool mouth, and the alarm of October.

Eleusinian Mystery

To make something of
the someone who isn't here with us

More to be made of
the someone who isn't here

Never enough made of
the someone who isn't

The someone who disappears
like the instar of a moth

The someone whose purpose
is to disappear

The someone who finds herself
disappearing

The someone whose purpose
is to appear

The someone whose purpose
is to appear speechless

The someone whose appearance
leaves us speechless

The someone whose appearance
is unspeakable

The appearance that leaves her
unspeakable

The appearance that leaves her

The appearance that leaves

The appearance

The Other Voice

It is said
the goal is not to climb the highest peak
but to master fear,
to find one's muscles in the most jagged spot,
the most exposed,
the climb mere practice for living
through the next earthquake.

Time and space contract
there,
the expanse of geology
reduced
to a topo map,
the mountain
reduced
to a body grown for the sake of discipline.

But might the goal also be to hear
the other voice
there,
the steady beat of the stone,
the pulse of magma
inching upward,
to understand
finally
the purpose of the planet
left
to creep
at its own pace,
the fault line's own
slow time.

Spelunking for Persephone

for Katie St. Clair, artist, spelunker

I can't imagine wedging myself between them,
this body of hips and back pressed against stone
to make me narrow enough to slide down into
the artery of bedrock, hoping for an opening.

Unlike you, I only enter stone through words,
this body unaccustomed to the resculpture of lungs,
the discipline of resizing the chest, as you phrase it,
breathing so slowed that oxygen hardly matters.

Whose chilled torso sweats from the exertion, yours,
or hers made of summer and winter at the same time?
Hers a body both almost alive and somewhat dead,
her liminal state to be dreaded, to be wholly desired.

What Hands Ask of Stone

a girl making her home in underground caverns
choosing to live in underground caverns
in underground caverns six months out of every year
why would a girl do that   before
she knows what it means to be   a woman
before she knows the mind of a woman
before she is that woman

a woman grooming her daughter
a woman knowing she grooms her daughter   for the underworld
a woman knowing   her daughter
will live in underground caverns
in underground caverns six months out of every year
why would a woman do that   knowing
her daughter will disappear into the underworld   before
she can become a woman

she becoming a woman   wondering
how her daughter
will come to have the mind of a woman
in the bowels of the earth
in a dark so dark she will not see
her own hands   touching
what they must
touching what women must   to become
things of the dark not needing
eyes for asking what hands do
in the early morning or afternoon or twilight of day

her underworld hands doing   nothing
to see the dark of the moon
hands in a dark so dark they need no eyes   to feel
what hands do
need no ears to hear
stone swallowing sound   needing
nothing but what hands ask of stone
her hands asking   nothing

God-Gathering Woman

She realized how indispensable she had become to him
when he stopped gathering souls one fall, sitting the next
spring by the scrying pool, stirring the seasons together.

The winter in between was business as usual for them
except there were no shades to witness the *hieros gamos,*
no up-above-world mourners to water the planted seeds.

She herself gathered the dying the following summer
when she understood that he had given himself over
completely, had given all his born-to-the-earth to her.

That year both domains and their several kingdoms
wondered at the strangeness, the seasons of the dead
compacted into one long heat wave, the world on fire.

Such was the moment Persephone stood naked, alone,
seeing herself as god-gatherer, balancing the demands
of the living against the mercurial nature of the Reaper.

Persephone's Curse

I keep trying
to forget her, or misremember.
When attempts at imagining myself with Alzheimer's fail,
attempts at telling her to go to Hell and stay there fail,
I fall headlong into the nearby lake she carved with a glacier,
not unlike the way I fell yesterday evening into the eye
of the Hunter moon
and wandered in its drug-wide iris all night long
from east to west,
warmed only by the exhale of the trees
rustling below me.

I know she uses me
as a tether to the color sugar maples make of their leaves,
just as I have used her for her eyes in the underworld,
but unlike her I didn't like what I witnessed there,
Hades that bruised shade of blue and her tears solid
as salt on my cheeks.

This morning,
with the moon in its hours of slivering off,
its slow-motion magician's act,
I still taste the blood she licked from the blade
after running with the deer,
her companions one last time
before she dragged their carcasses to the meat locker below,
where she stores what's left of her lover's body,
Hades frozen quite through now.

I see her
unable to stop force-feeding him through the winter,
unable to break the habit of her six-month retreat,
unable to let dead gods sleep in peace.

Persephone Refusing to Mourn

If its snapping jaw is any indicator,
the turtle escapes to another life
after its body has been stripped.

Hades, too, is still somewhere
about, the warmth of the stones
a reminder of his dragon breath.

And might this stony heat erupt
to the level of rival, competing
with the sun to nurture summer?

A summer to outface all seasons,
the land to melt like butter,
to sizzle at the touch of seas.

Hades' lava flowing everywhere,
his glowing arms to surround her,
to dress her in a molten world.

Signs of Life

How would she know if or
                    when
it was time to taste
                    again
the blood of pomegranate

Would the sign come
from the limbs of a bush
refusing to relinquish
                    leaves
to a floor's already thick
                    excess

Would the sign come
from within the stone
cold chamber that huddled
                    her
from the frost crouching
                    above

Would the sign come
from between these worlds,
the cave of her own mouth
                    open
to another body claiming her
                    kiss
or the worry of it

Bone Meal

Bone meal is the key
a dusty handful at the bottom of the hole
to be filled with the space that a tulip
                                    needs
to bloom itself above the earth's crust

Whose bones to crush
to plump that bulb's diameter up
to send its pale finger into the green
                                    reach
on the other side of the soil's gravity

Any bones will do
once a soul has escaped its thin skin
yearning for something else to be
                                    green
even at the expense of immortality

She Finds Herself Upworld in January

In a trippy coffee house,
a spontaneous human combustion
armchair
across from the couch she sits on
with the someone she can't think
to pin a name on,
words freezing between them.

Cracked faux leather
thin enough to show the fabric
facing of the chair,
thin enough for the stuffing to erupt
if accelerant were spilled there,
if someone would only
light a match.

Poinsettia on the mantlepiece
of a fake fireplace,
a theme developing here,
a wide mouth of stone,
a too-shallow cave,
a wilting plant to keep
watch,
all designed to keep someone
at a safe distance.

Earrings made of dyed stone
fish
dangling near the other mouth,
narrow smile on the human face,
someone out of season
meant for spring or summer
whatevers,
not this bulb cracking open
in January.

Enter Stone

I am stirred now
by the spirit slipping
from your skin,
ringing the stones
that stand for me

entered

stones that bind your
powers, fashioned
to work the flesh
that slides around
me sweet to sunlight

rippled

to the edge of you,
your power rings
stirred into my bones,
opened crack by crack
for me to enter stone

Ursa Major on a Clear Night

I always know what I want—untouchables—
skin hotter, harder, hungrier than my own,
bones dipped in the sublime, tempered there,
the knife of words, but a force never severing.

I have no proper words of courtship to woo,
to cliché me under your skin, into your blood.
With no lipstick to imprint me on your neck,
I covet the wax seal of a Renaissance doge.

Marlowe wrote "Come live with me and be
my love" because his winter lodge was empty,
because an unsanctioned baritone sent sound
waves through the air, thrumming his ribs.

Let us dare to cross-dress in our own fashion.
I would wear myrtle leaves trimmed in ichor.
And what might you wear? Mulberry cocoons?
Feather webs? A gyre of terra cotta dust?

If the air frightens us, where is left to go?
We are already masters of the underworld.
Let's journey, you and I, into some clouds,
the intangible finger of a cyclone to lift us.

First Cause

I will use you roughly.
I will drown you in
a glass of sweet wine,
such worthy drink
for a brimming world
of plump, firm fruit.

Ah, red, red apples,
juicing up and falling
two by two by two
from the tree, coupling
toward the flood of love.

I will eat them red
or eat them gold,
filling me with seeds
to sprout, to birth
upon the orchard floor.

Our progeny the seed
of stone, and I so thick
with heat and minerals
any heart to happen by
will turn to marble.

Adept, I juggle all,
passing hand to hand
round my breasts,
almost close enough
and never let one drop.

Surprising the God
of Motion

The Spider Talks to Her Creation

In Keresan mythology Ts'its'tsi'nako spins stories
out of her body, and her stories are the universe.

I settle my heavy body near the foundation
of your house
and thread me close to the dandelion star
you intend to kill
when the weather dries up
and the wind ends.

How to undo
your obsession with classifying green things
into crab or fruit,
weed or grass,
how to undo
the web, pull back time into my spinneret.

I wait for your foundation to crumble enough
to crack
into your basement
to thread some wild fragile leavings there
across the bottom
of your world.

Reading Tarot

I worry over the card I've turned,
like it might be bad theology
to assign to an empty tree
the meaning of a man
pitched from a Tarot pack,
swinging from a limb.

And the ambiguity of it,
feet feathered to the ground,
not quite a broken neck,
his atheism still holding,
half dangling like a leaf
still tethered to its twig.

No answer swings here,
only half-strangled questions,
how one could want to leap
to flimsy faith from a firm edge,
how my hand could itch
toward the next card.

Tiresias Among the Sycamores

Remember how it happened,
the inscrutable plan
against your singular direction?

When the sycamores found
blood between your legs
on that first day as a woman,
they took pity,
knowing the old story.

But you refused the dance
of broad leaves,
being disturbed enough having
to navigate the world in two
human bodies.

You still hear them call,
sycamore to sister,
knowing these sky-rubbing trees
speak in tongues beyond
the scrape they make of sky.

Do you know why
they bare their sage and birch
white arms longer
than other winter-loving trees?

Past the coziness
of hibernating dreams,
until summer's first heat,
they wait for you.

They dream your memory
of a man coming in
and a woman going out,
you bearing both.

They, the heart of green wood
that would take you for
their own
and dance the world
to full-blooming ambiguity
if you only would.

Things That Bite or Drag You Underground

giant ants or spiders in post-apocalyptic movies
a swarm of bees in your dreams
dragons, the real ones on the island of Komodo
dragonflies, if they are large enough

the hair of Medusa
Persephone, if you're lucky
Hades, if you're unlucky
or is it the other way around

spiders that crawl into your bed
bedbugs that make their home there
beds in houses constructed on faultlines
the planet, after its bowels have been fracked

the sound of a window breaking in the basement
the sound of one hand clapping over your mouth
the sound of a tree falling in the forest you fled to

words collapsing into vacuous questions like this
collapse into angels on the head of a pin

you, after you've demanded one-too-many miracles
me, after I've drunk too much consecrated wine

us, after we've eaten all the loaves and fishes
and buried the crumbs and bones under a myth

Castor and Pollux, after agreeing to disband Gemini
the solar system, after its star collapses into a black hole
the metaphor that a black hole always becomes

The God's Stone Mouth

Putting your hand in
       takes trust in
the god's stone mouth.

Let its teeth bite, kiss
       its tongue of fire
with your own, inhale.

Our lungs must burn
       away all oxygen,
fill with spirit's fission.

From our fiery lungs
       let magma flow
to the begging ocean.

Leaving the Skin Empty

Some of us are shy
about naming it,
this lust for something
taboo,
a divine someone in the bed.

Like the poet who pretends
to be gazing through
an invisible god
instead of at divinity's body,
afraid to admit the yearning
that, unacknowledged, shortens her life
a day for every day she lives
alone,
as if she can stop time's longing
by naming
and naming
and more naming of fellow
animals
instead of facing what can't be
named.

Clothing herself in words,
against desire for any naked god
who would be slipping,
ever slipping
out of bed
leaving the skin empty.

Scrying

Shadow scowls at me,
drops a tree's leaf-heavy limb
right in front of me.

Sudden clarity
hits me, storms me, roils in me,
exposes my want

just as the sky turns
gray with Shadow, heavy as
rain-soaked wool. I wait,

relax my fist as
rain shimmies down, unfolds me,
opens my palm to

whatever nut might
get dropped from the limb above
to my dim fate line.

Four Words of the Apocalypse

Omission

The best kind of lie contains the truth:
"I left you so I wouldn't have to kill you."

Ouroboros

What if Loki is no evil force,
merely self-preservation run amok.

Just before we destroy everything, the truth of it
revealed, the accident of intention.

Shiva's legs and arms the spidering out of creation
handy-dandy from beginning to end.

And don't think you're safe in the belly of a stone,
it too is destined to crack open from the inside.

Penultimate

February wind drifting into the howl of March
and other phenomena verging on extinction.

Anything that leapfrogs its fellow force
so as to win what it thinks is a competition.

Ricochet

The bullet in a brain case can ricochet for years
before the skull bursts from the pressure of blood.

You tell it like you were sleep walking,
the whole time dreaming of a rufous
hummingbird dive bombing your red hair
until you finally lost your temper,
slapped at her and she fell dead at your feet.

Except that it was you who got slapped,
your jaw cracking and something shifting
loose inside the way you think
about how men and women are supposed
to glue themselves to each other.

Something honest might come of this blood,
of you waking to the taste of metal,
the grit of bone fragments,
but only by putting your tongue to the floor
where the slick of you has pooled
for scrying the future.

Falling for the Cosmos

You are my obsession,
        you, soul's veneer.

You have made me
        into carnival,
my body clothed in
        the silk of you
swaying every way
        a leaf may.

I am wheat waving
        under the play
of wind, your puffings.

You nest me into you,
        a limestone cave
to shimmy into, to find
        shadow inside
shadow inside yet another
        shade of you.

I never tire of lying
        beneath you
on the grass at midnight,
        watching you
poke starry holes in
        your own body.

You let me clutch you
        as a child
keeps a rock collection,
        a river stone

caressed by little greedy
        hands needing
to own a firm surface,
        only to crack
it apart with a hammer.

It . . . you . . . cracked
        into shards
willingly, willfully.

Your trick, sharding me
        apart as you split.

Me splitting as I fall
        into texture,
me craving ever more of
        the silk,
the sandpaper sky
        of you.

Trusting the Serpent

She tells me not to be
deceived,
that my prayers against
darkness
should not be against Shadow,
not against
writhing holiness licking
human shores,
fertilizing home-plantings
with energy,
playing its tempest trickster
games
by the light of my homegrown
fire.

She assures me of the safety
of trust
in the paradox of this shadowy
vision,
this sweetwater flame dancing,
encircling me
and my doubting greenwood
smolder,
singeing skin with bone-licking
acid
even as it stitches dragon wings
to my arms,
this thick leather to clothe me
against
my own soul-chilling light.

Thirteen Versions of the Big Bang

The story of the god says "I am an observer story
as well as a creator story, wide-ranging in my
affection, my despite, my indifference engendering
all emotional states, then stepping back to watch
them play out. But while I take credit for it all,
don't expect any story of duty or loyalty out of me,
for I tell the story of you and you and you and
all your permutations simply for myself, this my
urge, this my raison d'être."

Use
this
space
to
tell
your
own
story.

The story of the lost soul says "I need you to be this
one story, no other. Make it be my story that
matters. Make me matter. Make me into matter."

The story of the baby says "wah, wah, wah," and
that could mean just about anything.

The story of the bloody knife says "I just wanted
you to love me, if you had loved me, I could have
been good to you, why couldn't you have loved me,
why can't I cut you tenderly, you make me crazy,
if only you had loved me."

The story of fire says "I burn, you burn, we all burn. Ashes. Ashes."

The story of the extinct house says "I simply grew too old to bear the weight of rafters. I'm sorry for how brittle my bones became, sorry you were inside my ribcage when I collapsed, sorry I couldn't have given you warning, sorry my extinction caused yours. Truly, I didn't know I was about to tumble down to smothering rubble till I did. We were all just fine until we weren't."

The story of apocalypse says "Satyagraha is enough, this holding onto the truth of story, no flight or fight but the standing firm, looking story in the eye even as it pierces you through your own eye, into the heart of your story."

The story of truth says "What hubris, what folly to attempt the story of Truth."

The story of the snowman says "One must have a mind of winter to behold the fine intellect of the Stevensian landscape, to revel in the bare wind, its tree-stripping howl, its misery, its hunger, without despair, hearing in winter's hollow the laughing story of summer."

The story of the farmer says "Who knows why, I don't know, maybe I'm just lucky, never really thought about it, just go out there every day and plant those rows, somebody's got to do it, and the dirt is clean and always smells like something's about to sprout."

The story of the crusty dishes in the sink says "It's not safe with you two in the kitchen, dancing the can-can, shaking the spice rack like a California earthquake. The paprika on the spice rack could have fallen and cracked one of us. Then where would we be? A mess of broken, dirty dishes . . . and wipe those goofy grins from your faces."

If you haven't
told your story
by now,
it might be
too late,
I hope not,
for without it
we're missing
the twelfth
version of
the Big Bang.

The story of the snake in the grass says "Did you ever even try to pick me up? I'm not slimy at all, and my flicking tongue is soft as a kiss on your cheek. By it I know you and your story. But how have you known me except by the story told by an old jealous god? Don't be too quick to believe his version."

Ashes, Ashes

The gods lie to us as they must,
and we to them.

How many demons can spin arms outstretched
on the head of a pin?

All of them.
All of us.

Spinning dizzy drunk until we all fall
into the inevitable

crucible, all spindly spines and wobbly wings
melted down to aspic.

Who to be responsible for all this mutability,
a god or us?

Ashes, ashes
the question of cause.

The Shame of It

The sin of Orpheus was not to look back,
        this the mere distrust of a mercurial god,

or mere self-doubt of the candor it takes
        to face and claim life in the lock of eyes,

the eyeful of his beloved, wrongfully taken,
        willfully returned, thumbing at destiny.

The sin was in looking away in shame
        after seeing and being seen, naked,

and after that, to let the lord of dark and dank
        hollows exercise dominion over them.

Job, Fresh from Apotheosis

Rich in naked finery you fall
fresh from apotheosis
back to your tribe on earth.

Here you are more welcome
than any starry eye
of the maker's face,
that face the trick of
a long-dead science,
the alchemy of
a jealous old sadist
with a head too big
to be photographed,
blowing tornadoes
to gyre honest folk
toward cold pasteboard stars.

When he makes wondrous lies
of his awful
disembodiment,
you believe him,
accord him your own
generous intelligence,
ask your progeny
to do likewise,
a continued charity,
this gift of generations
to a beggar thought
still hungering
for your fine blood and bones.

Potter's Retreat, Poet's Ground

The lure of swamp fire and promise
of a land edging west of every god,

where the fat heads of winter wheat sit on
stalks grown thick enough to withstand
any late spring hailstorm of Ohio,

where I pitch my tent on Indiana ground
swept clean of stones, and hear the echo
that rain makes when it hits a shale outcrop,

where the offspring of last summer's
dragonflies emerge by the dozens to guide
would-be potters up a hill to a beehive kiln,

where words that buzz loose in the mouth
are given over to the clay that made the world,

where the wood burning in the campfire
reminds me of why I want to live forever.

Ts'its'tsi'nako

The weaver may measure your shroud,
the scissors of the three Fates snipping
the wormy silk of the mulberry tree.

Yet Creation is still the thread of a spider,
her legs plucking strings of the universe.

The angel may quiver into your chest,
a feather stirring the blood to a froth,
bringing the heart to the boiling point.

Still, rebellion makes a good lover,
Lucifer needing only a shared vision.

The trickster may slip into your bed,
Oden wooing with an elixir of youth,
a vial as precious to lovers as naïveté.

But belief still ferments in the marrow
of the bone, where fat can last forever.

Reporting What Appeared,
Surprising the God of Motion

I

cloud-to-cloud lightning
thirsting for a body to detonate.

II

a mountain's exposed copper deposits
electrified at the timberline,
raising the hackles of hikers just clearing the trail,
setting twisted Bristlecone Pine ablaze,
setting the hikers into frantic motion
fleeing up the slope
to seek shelter on the summit,
knowing the folly of their logic,
climbing to the top of the world,
exposing themselves to the possibility of hell
on the off chance of meeting heaven there,
their bodies forgetting terror,
thrilling at the prospect of exploding
in the bare white light.

III

a couple who fell out of love yesterday
pretending it didn't happen,
willing their bodies to respond to each other,
accustomed to the habits of love,
accustomed to the decades of companionship
causing them to go through the motions
as if they were still twenty-somethings,

trusting in the rebirth of the body's urge,
surely just a matter of waking after sleep,
tomorrow waking in the same bed,
waking to the promise of chemistry
stirring heat into them.

IV

the wall of a Brooklyn garden
shielding bushes of black roses
blooming for a woman who is ever
craving the colors of night,
seeking the shade of the full moon and
hoping to become its consort,
groaning in jealousy at the sight of petals
that reflect the moon's white light,
begging for a share of grace
as they dance with the spider web
that spans the distance between bush and wall and
reminds her of the rapture of weightlessness,
the gravity of her skin suddenly inconsequential
as she competes with a spider for a sliver of heaven.

V

the side street near the wall
of that same Brooklyn garden,
absorbing the black of night
beneath the house of the bleached-out woman
who ignores the schizophrenic man rooted to concrete
conversing with his god of the sidewalk,
casting his spell of spells to cut
midnight into a million shards,
his mouth dazzling with perfect words
for escaping the stump of his grimy body,

dismissing the wasted thing,
dismissing the story of wasting in the house above,
even dismissing the story of loving the colorless woman
though the taste of her still effervesces
on his tongue
burning from the blessed wafer's dissolution.

VI

a wildfire claiming the prairie,
searing the skin of the planet
that spins its denizens toward the ecstasy of nonbeing,
its thirsty body burning to live.

VII

the bed of a paraplegic,
dreaming the thirst of thirsts,
dreaming of swimming in a tank of his own tears,
his legs scissoring through the salt water,
remembering the muscle's automatic motion,
dreaming his body at last emptied into
forgiveness for all the drunk drivers of the world,
waking from the dream in his kitchen
standing at the sink,
running cold water over his wrists,
cupping his hands under the stream,
bending to drink from the pool they have made,
realizing his spine and legs have found a way
to revise the story his body has been inhabiting,
surprising the god of motion.

Earning
Apocolypse

Where It Begins

Where it begins is the chatter of teeth,
the uncontrollable rattle of shoulders.

Where it begins is a hand nesting in wool
to steal warmth from an animal's skin.

But let's take a step back, or to the slant,
a dead sheep in sight, a razor-sharp flint.

Where it begins is the sheep's cold body
and a hand itching to carve something.

Where it begins is a hide made to defy
the ice, a warm human wrapped inside.

A Murder of Crows

They watching us in their territory,
judging the latex masks we wear,
our experiment on them, theirs on us,
testing each other's aptitude
for facial recognition.

Our surveillance of them a game played
in a house of mirrors,
regression to that primal urge to murder
the one whose image recurs
as far as the eye can see itself,
as sharp as the blade of a wing.

The foreboding music of horror flicks
sounding like the "caw caw caw"
that flaps overhead
as we spy them spying us,
wings spread so wide and high
the sky stutters between feathers,
a murder of crows no less than
a murder of humans below.

On Seeing, Too Close

Chelydra serpentina is not to be mistaken for a snake,
despite the look of its head erupting from an accordion neck.
It is the fierce-clamping jaw that does all the damage;
it is the cold eye, the hiss just before it springs and snaps.

Because the head can erupt from its accordion neck,
my father warned "stand back" while reaching for his axe.
The cold eye and hiss just before it sprang and snapped
was all the confirmation I needed, this affirmation of dread.

My father warned "stand back" while reaching for his axe.
My brother hefted a hook and chain, taunted the thing to strike,
these the confirmation I needed to shock me out of my dread
and jump to the side before it could snap through my leg.

My brother hefted the sharp-toothed hook, taunted it to strike,
and as the snapping turtle's neck sprang, steel found home,
and I jumped to the side, my leg escaping jaw and hook.
But the turtle's head escaped neither hook nor axe,

for when a snapping turtle's neck springs, steel will find home
in a soft eye, out a mouth. My brother pulled the chain taut,
and thus the turtle's head escaped neither hook nor the axe
my father lifted and let drop in the practiced ritual that it was.

In the eye, out the mouth, the hook at the taut chain's end
held the head as still and ready as a martyr for the axe
my father lifted and let drop in the practiced ritual that it was,
severing the head, leaving jaws to snap as if in afterthought.

The head held still and ready as a martyr for the axe,
the turtle's jaw snapped, snapped again as if a living severed
head. But snapping jaws are nothing more than afterthought,
C. serpentina not to be confused with these snaking words.

No Human Words

I have seen bald eagles perched on trees above the Apgar bridge
but that poem has already been written: the splendor of those raptors,
wings wide enough to hug the nearby glacier-scoured mountain,
claws lifting Kokanee salmon high above their spawning run.

How to speak of a lone golden eagle spanning the Big Empty sky,
its domain the vast above and below of sagebrush territory,
its home snugged within branches packed into a cleft,
the cliff aerie cupping its chick, the center of its world,

its partner with taloned meat, shredding morsel after morsel
for their eaglet, now fledging the feathers that will take it
to the edge of the universe and beyond, where no staccato call
of a parent, no chirping whistle, no human words can ground it.

Romantic Tone

As if nuthatches were designed
by the laws of evolution
by the categories of ontology
by the breath of the divine
for the express purpose of
providing atmosphere for me.

My human cry projected into
their eight-note voicings
as I take the local tow path or,
rather, it takes me for a walk
to clear my head of all fellow
members of the human species.

Why would I burden such
little birds with the folly
of the seven billion of us.

Why continue to toss
my romantic tone at their
blue-gray bodies.

As if they should bear
the weight of sympathy
for even one of us.

Mapping Protean Things

because of Romulus Whitaker

I scan the Hereford Mappa Mundi, wishing I could see it
at the cathedral, having to settle for an internet tourist site.

Crown one's hometown the center of the universe, and old
topo maps will reveal the earth's shapeshifter properties.

Here, the Garden of Eden appears at the top, encircled
by Africa and Europe, chummy cross-pollinating bodies.

Their transposable progeny delight in dragon chronicles
of an African maid saved by a Turkish St. George.

Each dragon chronicle stories us to the world before
we had talked ourselves into slaying our brothers.

The last baby dragon, the olm of Postojna, frills its gills
to prove the magic of fire and water cohabiting.

A cave has saved this atavist of the fire breather,
its survival a matter of geology and human nostalgia.

Unlike the neck-frilled dragon lizard of Australia,
its frill and colored mouth a shock to any challenger.

Let the olm trade on stories of man-eating dragons,
old African tales of appeasing them with plump maidens.

The Mappa Mundi trades on the still-comfortable illusion
of a flat world and a sharp separation of spirit and body.

If only our corpus callosum could bridge actual land masses
with those myth lands only seen out of the corner of the eye.

Ah, to be a bumblebee, to see Earth straight on and pin it
down with a narrow tongue, but a thousand times shifted.

A bumblebee's tongue can slide into a morning glory
shuttered tight at night and sip its nectar without damage.

Any mythic dragon's tongue goes unnoticed, a mere
remnant of evolution into a frog licking up mosquitoes.

But this little-known fact remains unrecorded to this day,
neither in encyclopedia nor on the great Mappa Mundi.

The oversight perhaps a matter of our medieval world
with its appetite for fiery breath, talons, and stingers.

Bees, wasps, dragons, lizards, amphibians, dragonflies
all look alike when viewed through eyelids pressed tight.

Pressure on the eyelid excites a glow behind the lid,
press long enough and the sting of it flares to fire.

Press long and hard on skin stung by a wasp or bee
and the fire of it dissipates, fire to ember to charcoal.

Bands of *Homo sapiens* squatted around fires, tossing
their stories of near-death into the fringe of embers.

Like my uncle telling of shooting a bushmaster's head off,
its seven-foot hide now locked in a chest in our basement.

Once upon a time my sister was entertained in Abu Dhabi,
was seated on the cushion of honor near a bowl of milk.

A cobra silenced through the room, the transmigrated soul
of the matriarch, to lap up milk at the head of the table.

The cobra spits watery venom into the eyes of an enemy
to burn a hole in Eden, to drill through the world's crust,

To force open the shuttered golden spiral of the universe,
to demand obeisance to death robed in its leathery scales.

The spread of the cobra's hood seduces me, but it's the spit
of poison that keeps me, for whose eye can turn from fire.

Though we burn from learning the dragon's way, who
can turn from the blood-red gills in the dragonfly's lair?

A triple seduction, I think, to complete Eden's cross-
pollination, to clothe the body in fire, to slay our source.

And so I peer at maps of protean things, maps to lost glories,
unable to turn away, wondering where fire will strike next.

Blue Crow Eyes

Before a crow's eyes change from blue to black
she admits to seeing the grief of her species,
the death of siblings a required easement,
so those left behind might have nest and food.

We admit to seeing the grief of her species,
we pause with the omnivore's understanding
that those left behind must have food and nest,
the twigs placed and laced by symmetry's law.

We pause with the omnivore's understanding,
a murder of crows has an engineer's mind,
the twigs placed and laced by symmetry's law,
a rake for gathering, hook for threading.

A murder of crows has an engineer's mind,
using beak and claw for shaping their tools,
a rake for gathering, hook for threading,
but nothing but wings to hide their grief.

Using beak and claw for shaping a tool,
one may own the world. But a crow must know
there's just her wing to hide her grief
before her eyes change from blue to black.

Nox, Rain

The best rains come at night
just after I've zipped myself
into the tent.

Shoes under the shelter
of the fly, feet dry,
mosquito buzz on the net's
other side.

The first drop a ping,
the call to all fellow
rain to dive.

Bodies in free fall,
their staccato suicide
humming into the tent,
consolatio.

Earning Apocalypse

Against the skylight itself, with a cymbal-like buzzing,
thousands of insects clustered in a golden mob. . . .
from my cobwebbed old garret, I thrust forth my head
into the balmy air.

—Herman Melville, "The Apple-Tree Table"

I

I philosophize ant biomass
citing its parallel to human mass
some psychic connection perhaps
some spiritual bond between
superorganisms held in balance by Gaia herself.

I poeticize bee colonies
making of them a metonymy for the hive of humans
a stand-in for our industry
our ripening passions
our communal designs
a poster child of us.

I fail, I fail, I fail
to see the fact of insects having their own eyes
following their own somatic moods
their own evolutionary gestures
their own smell
beyond all philosophy.

II

Apocalypse, unlike resurrection, is an earned thing
coming at a cost
a Lazarus who has been buried and claws his way
out of the ground
his upward travail
through six feet of earth providing time to lay bare

a new code to live by
the revelation complete at the precise moment
his fingers break free.

Apocalypse, every instar of the silkworm moth needed
for its bedazzlement
the revelation process not limited to the final silk cocoon
but spread across five
white naked bodies.

Apocalypse, the story of a man compelled to tell the tale
of a bug trapped in a table
erupting from the wood after a century of interment
the man in awe
thinking it a miracle.

Apocalypse, surely a moment of breaking free for
the man caught in the cobwebs
of his old building's garret
insects flying round his head
a narrow ladder leading upward to a narrower window
opening to the roof
to the unwebbed universe.

The Grammar of Apocalypse

The children of frogs taught me the grammar of apocalypse
when I was small
and squatting in the shallows of Sawlog Creek, there
in the shade of a cottonwood, my hands dyed
green from the noonday sun filtered through spring leaves,
and wet from plowing the water, tadpoles in the wake

of fingers spread wide. I was a child, not yet awake
to the ways of the universe, but alive to anything I put my lips
and nose and fingers to: the water, a nearby frog, the leaves
of grass, all within a small
body's reach, a body edging near adulthood, dying
to be born into that cabal, to know what everybody there

knew of how things grew, of the beginning of life there
in my mother's nearby belly, of the way you could wake
the dead if you lived in a long-ago story where people died
of leprosy spreading across the skin like apocalypse . . .
or was it like snow. My small
mind could not keep words and things straight, the leaf

of a tree being the same thing as my favorite color, a leaf
sure to taste like green Jell-o, or so I imagined their
flavors the same, until I chewed a small
leaf one day, shortly before the day when tadpoles wakened
in me the question of why their frog mothers have lips
and lungs but they do not. Do pollywogs have to die

for their gills to disappear, die for their legs to sprout, die
as their tails dissolve away to nothing and leave
behind the ways of fish? It took weeks for that apocalypse,
one life meandering to its end, another beginning there
at the inner bend of the creek, and in that time I felt the quake
of change in my own small

body, stepping beyond smell
and touch and taste, seeing the texture of pigments that dye
my world to a thing called color, being shaken fully awake
to voices that once were mere backdrop. Still today they leave
me both troubled and aroused, ripened to the meaning of their
murmur. I know that reach for air as gills disappear, the apocalypse

of each live thing. The small daily steps to larger geometries leave
me humble to the cast of the die, the way the living sleep in their
nests and dens and beds, trusting to wake as surely as the frog leaps.

A Map to Live On

In the protected territory
of dreams
the mandibles coming at me,
chewing my edges clean
of years of debris,
the smoking lean-to of nightmares
dribbled with water,
mixed into paste,
daubed into holes
of memories best left behind.

In the protected territory
of a cupola,
safe from heavy weather
under an eave,
in a furnace exhaust,
in the open cavity of a porch lamp,
my single six-sided cell
the beginnings of a nest
of masticated wood
stripped from a fence
weathered free of paint,
an old shed,
a flower lattice,
the pulpy mud
drying paper thin.

In the protected territory
of a story
a wasp perforating me
down the middle,
the needle punching a straight line
of uniform holes,
letting in pinprick light
between the two sides
of an amorphous golem,
the design of a map to live on.

Turning to Stone

It was while hiking Lizard Head in the San Juan range—we
already above timberline and skirting a talus field below the
vertical summit, coming around a large angular rock—that I saw
it, a common yellow-bellied rodent in the scree, a marmot.

As I stopped to photograph it, expecting it to crouch, to scurry
to a burrow, it remained fully upright on its hind legs, puffing
its chest fur out as if to say, "here I am, what's it to you."

My thoughts tumbled—surely it heard the whistle of colony
mates, safe from view, camouflaged by tawny brown coats
and white trim.

What instinct must be at work, that body drawn upright
to enlarge itself, that expanse of chest and arm muscle,
that bodybuilder's frontal pose.

Surely it intuited me as a predator—the sudden appearance
of my mane, my long red hair like the foxes and coyotes
in the area—and yet it was fearless, staring me down.

A good response given its low position on the food chain.

Forgetting the camera in my hand, I was enthralled, studying
its face like a believer peering into a stone whose cracks
and shadows look eerily like a saint's eyes, begging for faith.

The only response left to one already turned to stone.

Tracking a Grizzly

Imagine huckleberry season up at Glacier Park, the whole
gang of us tramping through white spruce, Douglas fir,
hemlock, spongy needles beneath our feet.

Our muffled progress toward the shrubs, their roots
in soil opened by fire decades ago, the bodies of trees
seeking the immortality of sky.

We didn't forget jingle bells, pulled from the Christmas
box to bracelet our wrists, to announce our theft
to the grizzly, her food to be taken for winter pies.

But we are not apt to startle her anyway, she knowing
who trespasses her lands, she bestowing patience on us,
the stringy creatures who sit on their butts just like her.

Imagine what she'd think being put on a protected species
list, what she might like to do to our colorful cloth hides,
how she might like to lick our blueberry-purple fingers.

Imagine her watching us close the lids on plastic boxes
filled with her fruit, imagine her tracking us as we hike
toward the stand of great western cedars.

Her looking up as we do, up the bark of the last old
cedars, these few protected from the chainsaw's bite.
Her wondering what to do with us.

To Shed Skin

Wasps at the door kept me closed behind it
until at least fifteen, me finally practicing courage.

Timidity gave way to heel-skating an avalanche
of gravel, Centennial Peak's cliff just to the left.

But when our dog stalled at something in the willow
copse ahead, we moused back down the trail.

To my jealousy, other hikers reported the grizzly
eyeing them as if puzzled by their copse whacking.

Another poet walked to her cabin as a cougar
toyed with her dress, stripping her naked.

But when the cat on Hermosa Cliffs startled me,
we both ran, neither of us ready to be touched.

I tell myself Tiresias separated copulating snakes,
look what he gained trading his body for wisdom.

So when the python in my garden swallows her
rat whole, I satisfy my urge to stroke her belly.

Oh, Animals! More dangerous than any geologic
fall of three thousand feet near a crumbling peak.

Yet more thrilling, like the walk from the cabin
to the woods at two a.m., finding a just-right spot,

squatting half-naked, and hearing something next
to me, the grunt of the neighborhood bear's sleep.

In such moments, to be a snake shedding its skin.

On Seeing Beyond

It might be the dragonfly in the swampy yard just
outside my bedroom doors making it happen,
scrimming my eyesight through its wings
—through my idea of its haze of wings—
holding my cornea's gaze with eyes that see
everywhere at once,
see everything at once,
its iridesce the magnet that lures me to look,
its deliberate hover a tether.

It might be the hummingbird moth that rested
on my neighbor's butterfly bush seven years ago,
that slipped its proboscis into the underside
of my eye socket and into my brain,
where it probes for nectar to this day,
activating images of itself every time it journeys
into my occipital lobe,
its touch of temporal lobe
reminding me that we hummed together once,
it still humming there,
in one of the cells of my mind.

It might be the hundreds of baby praying mantises
tumbling from their egg sac on that same
butterfly bush,
that same year,
crawling from branch to branch,
bush to bush,
until they reached the overgrown sprays
greening my front door,
folding their front legs together,
their prayer mine as soon as I opened it.

It might be the earwigs crawling out of the lump
of terra cotta shards and dry potting soil,
dumped from the clay pot I was planning
to use for this summer's impatiens,
they reminding me that bodies can be snatched
from the inside,
for everyone knows how
an earwig crawls into the ear,
tunnels along the nerve strands,
into the brain,
and deposits its eggs
to incubate and bloom there,
someplace just beyond consciousness.

It might be the baby spider just now dropping
from the lamp edge onto my table,
the circle of light barely inside the vertical silk
line it cuts and leaves behind
as it fingers its way
across the black hardback cover
of a book about its cousin ant,
meandering to the edge of this flat world,
and over the side,
going somewhere for now,
going everywhere someday,
its fuzzy legs a surrogate for mine,
a proxy for my totter.

To Belong

I

the green man at our door, his bold invitation
to dance a forest into being

his leafy skin, paper-thin
wrappings of primordial plenty

his magic, to tune us to our planet

II

fluted bone, this phrase suggesting music
as if our bones could be played

their microscopic ridges
evoking the glacial grooves at Kelleys Island

created by nature's artist, ice on stone

III

a committee of bees, their science instructive
beyond hive maintenance

our species might yet learn to dance intrications
of round and waggle

to be implicated, to belong

The Untamed
Grave of Us

Private Records

Our public records, yours and mine,
what is left of us: birth certificates,
marriage license, dissolution decree,
our state having civilized divorce.
If anything, we put on a civilized front,
putting aside the stories that expose,
if not explain, our joint privacies.

We hold each other, our own selves,
separate, willfully forgetting old intimacies,
like covering a roasted bird with a dome,
or the Victorian grotesque of putting
trousers on piano legs for modesty's sake.
We have left the camera used on vacation
back in Montana on our mountain haunt.

There should have been photos to show
our grandchildren, us posed beneath
lodgepole pine, your guitar in hand,
me sitting on an overstuffed backpack,
our bodies tucked behind the creases
of hiking shirts and pants, revealing
the ecology of what we wanted to be, us.

Marble Love

How much better for them both,
that crazy mad Othello
to have been right in his surmise,
his saintly Desdemona
to have taken a lover after all.

But no man could get inside
that sad mad-in-love woman
the way her taciturn soldier could,
so let's make a story not to be
refused, it's all in the phrasing:

Propriety meets sublime whisper,
a museum's unwashed art,
a naked Roman god tempting,
and she's as easily conquered as
her man lured by Iago's purr.

Seduction's all about the voice,
the best of the Hellenistic god is
its mouth seeking her raw heart,
the marble love's polished beg
for her strawberry handkerchief.

Never Having to Feel Gratitude

It was to be
simply to be
             paradise.

We never having
             to feel gratitude
for the difference made
by a cloud's shadow
crossing the lake
you and I happened
             to be
swimming in.

We never outside
             peering in
to each other's eyes.

You never being
             separate
from me.

We never needing to be
             some thing
to one another.

We never needing
to need
             any thing.

Never needing
to seize
             love.

Never Penetrate

I meant to pull you through
the tiny cracks forming
on your forehead
pull you through
to the room where you and I
are naked with our eyes open

I found that all those cracks
are webbings wrapped around
your stony face
webbings shot across
your frozen head
webbings I may shimmy up
but never penetrate

What This Must Mean

I know what this must mean,
only now noticing our shoes,
mismatched all these years,
your polished leather dress shoes,
my high-top hikers caked with dried mud.

I know what this must mean,
picturing you as water
shed through cupped hands,
me leaving the proverbial water hole
headed for my forty days in the desert.

I know what this must mean,
turning myself into a survivalist
armed with the folded photograph
of one left behind because he could not
stomach the sandy taste of dehydrated love.

Looking Like Frostbite

This dry summer sun finally bleached the mold
the alien colony that settled on your skin
thriving through the winter
your body the only warm place
in the seven empty rooms bound together
by tight-closed doors
our home
that shell around unheated eyes
my eyes or yours or both, who could tell
for we were equal in the game of silence.

No matter who stared the longer
we both survived
the colony of longing that fed
on the surface of us.

We ate just enough for heat
enough to sustain us without having to touch
too much
while watching the bloom of white
spread up your arms
down your chest, belly, thighs
—or was it I who blossomed leprosy—
looking like frostbite
should look to naked eyes
before the skin blackens.

Our awful patience lasted through
frost-encrusted windowpanes
through solstice and equinox
the scrub of spring.

You'd think we would be happy
to see the cure of it.

The Untamed Grave of Us

The light fixture swung above your head
—some hue between white and yellow
luminosity in the squashed sphere—
a hazy fixture to my eyes
because I'd given up my glasses to the table
beside our bed.
I imagined opaque light shimmering to a wraith
behind convex eyes . . .
and your face attracted me.

Your teeth lurked, waiting for an opportunity
—shadowed by your open lips—
and you could not see the light behind,
only me watching it spread thinly above.
Neither did you notice
the lily that I'd sewn,
one calla lily needlework hanging on the wall
to your right . . .
out of sight.

I traced the lines curving down the white petal
—really a bleached leaf—
to the base
with my index finger in the air
never daring to touch the still life,
the sea green leaves and circle of black ground.
I imagined laying lilies on the untamed
grave of us . . .
but still your face attracted me.

Your blue eyes framed by half-white teeth
and wrinkled brow

—diagonal rays extending from a point
originating between your eyes—
you never blinking
never breaking the sweeping gaze
slowed seconds from me
sweeping outward ...
your emergence glazed.

And I imagined being in and of your eyes
—squinting out of flattened mind—
never blinking once,
inverted irises and concave heart
now emptied of desire,
a radiation spent and growing cold
dead as winter moon and frozen stars
unblinking ...
and still it was your face.

Sour Things

Cultivating distance, like a gardener
tending evenly spaced tomato plants

this harvest of empty rooms
and unused bed against a bare wall

the wall clock bearing silence
for three-fourths of every second

it must have been more than
you biting into that crab apple

then kissing me, knowing
I hate the taste of sour things

Old Love, Old Objects

Blood-red leather, old
gloves worn paper-thin
mended three times past our six thousand days
your gift presented late one winter night
reading tossed aside
easy naked you easy naked me.

Smooth jasper sliver
from our mountain trail
erosion's companion
how to remainder this opaque stone
where to find a buyer
to love it, to give
dispensation from our obligations
uneasy you uneasy me.

Dime in the bathroom tank
thrown in for luck
found after fifteen years of solitude
its face worn off
its silver long gone
its copper body dripping
with possibility
something new in something old.

Embroidery

Camping out on this side of the sphinx,
crisscrossed by vinyl-coated hardware
interface wires, dotted with toggles
flipped to the magnet side of the sky,
we overreach the magic of electricity,
we techies of the twenty-first century.

Even so, I like to imagine your hands
upon my face, both of them the smoky
gray shade of silicon dioxide, darkened
by the virtual sun of the LED for so
long that silicon and plastic encase us
like black varnish on desert sandstone.

I like to think our binary landscape
is body-friendly, but my mouth is
parched as we set up camp beside
the pixel-sphinx and trek for days
in our old raggedy protocols,
looking for the magic code of codes.

I dream the desert sand is burning my
eyes, instead of my own blinkless stare
into a faceless light twenty-two inches
from a nose that no longer remembers
the scent of roses or other embroideries
of flower, food, and human pheromones.

When logic fails, our program looping
back upon itself, what Happy Fall to
exit our ouroboros, forget the riddle.

Confession, To Desire Objects

To be a mere object of another's desire
and not particularly disturbed by it
not disturbed by my own greed
for the mementos of trysts—gifts
a pair of jade earrings
a first edition of *Sword Blades*
and Poppy Seed.

A dozen blood-red roses—desire
for these objects greater than any need
of companionship
especially when it means another body
strapped to mine.

Another body sliding across my bones
such a simple act
such a powerful act—dangerous
as if lips might suddenly mutate
into sharp stropped edges
leave scars
inside the breastbone.

No such mementos to be left behind
on the skin—tattoos
being gifts that demand too much.

My solar plexus remains
untouched—empty
center of the universe.

Miriam, Bitter Sea

Is this the only body that counts now,
these disarticulated bones of the skull
stripped of flesh, fitted with sockets?
One technology supplanting the last,
the plow rusting in a virtual field now,
dead steel jacked into a state of pure
will to power, forging the idea of
something new under an old, old sun.

However fresh-seeming such desire,
this old CPU is bound to a green sea,
bound to taste the bitter, salty foam,
ever swimming toward a shifting beach,
breathing in the deep organic language
as familiar as the soil, the sky, the water,
this flood of nostalgia for a garden free
of apples, fig leaves, and original sin.

Compulsions, Still

Compulsions, still to be shared after all
these decades,
a matter of habit

probably

a matter of the communication that brought you
into first sight
or into olfaction,
such signals having little to do with eyes

perhaps

the same ineluctable pheromone that gave me
your dreams,
especially the ones that caused night terrors,
yours and mine at the same time

possibly

as much to do with my greenstick collar break
as the abraded neck of your childhood,
the small noose tied out of a tea towel
by your own hands

maybe

your compulsion to choke out the world still
the best companion for me,
one still trying to gather all the words
thrown out of her, scattered

still

A Sycamore's Touch

Dear Sycamore in my ex-lover's side yard,

                    This is just to let you know
it was the apprehension of touch—not the actual touch,
when it finally arrived—that made all the difference.

Duration also mattered—like foreplay making the
difference
                between two people
attending to one another before getting lost inside, before
                their beings split from
each other for the sake of individual fullness, for the
expanse
that wandering alone inside brings—measurable by how
many fissioning seconds my arm hair remained standing.

Your actual touch felt like a waxed-paper wrapper blown
by a gusty wind—I tested the naming of this sensation
against
                the wind itself,
against my own breath, against office paper brushing my
arm,
even the feeling of a light cotton sweater—across my arm,
                gone the next moment.

Giving it this much thought keeps it—a heavy feedback loop
of sorts—happening, though you haven't rocked me in
that way
                for years and years.

Life with the Green Man

I never needed
my god to be a hero,
only a good man,

gentle in his heart
with eyes green from gardening,
mud-dirtied fingers,

legs of plane tree trunks,
strong roots feeding his mind, high
with me in the sky,

where all dreams hover,
where the music of the spheres
finds its perfect pitch.

Sin of the Cyborg

I would the universe to gather,
a celebration of apples
eaten hungrily two by two,
women feasting together,
a glut of tooth marks,
men facing their bodies
untouched by fig leaves,
and each testing knowledge,
the difference between
the sin of an empty mouth
and the earned innocence
of once-dormant seeds
spit from sated lips
to the rich black loam,
strong roots snaking
into rain-soaked ground,
and leaves shooting up
as fast as a star can
explode into the white
light of apple blossoms.

Cancer Wine

Caul eater, crawl
inside my belly
to remind me
how I hunger.

Spider mum,
germinate
in my mouth
to bless my kiss.

Cancer wine,
bloom across
my cheeks like
the blush of sex.

Thin grey blade,
skin me alive
else I forget
pain in desire.

Word Monsters

I

Today I may finally be untwined from you,
word monster,
my secret name for you, I now recognize
my name as well.

My body a tangle of knots, a nest of
words meant to resolve
but muddle-stitched in contrary directions,
ambivalence pulled taut.

Speech, however precise, at cross purposes,
an over-threaded ball
stuck in the gut, with no clean complaint
to scissor out.

II

Yesterday we were both rain-seeking ruin,
pothole puddles.

The dribble noise that bloodletting makes
as we victim-sigh.

The flood-loving body throwing itself
into thunder's song.

III

Tomorrow let's clean mudded shoes,
bleach blooded sheets,
swallow down all these empty words.

To Invent What We Desire

The story is based on you and me
during that foolhardy hour,
or was it an hour of courage,
the time it took for our plot to cool
beside the once-hot Darjeeling.

The paradox that once the words
are out, they don't belong to us,
that this desire for a faithful lover
is a ripple delivered by my breath
but not the breath itself.

The tea's surface flutters,
returns to its own mood.

The conventions of invention,
necessity of fantasy, the nerve
to say why it matters to place
a hand on a dangerously hot body.

Or to imagine the hand there,
my boldness a borrowed thing,
your frank eyes on loan
for that hour, the syntax
of desire sufficient unto itself.

The tea's surface flutters,
returns to its own mood.

The Found Object
Imagines a Life

Imagining Life as a Graffiti Artist

for Steve Smith, potter,
generous Midwestern artist

"Art is not a crime"
he tells us gesticulating.

"Art is not a crime"
his words reverberating through
the drab lecture hall.

"Art is not a crime"
this spray painted on a streetside wall
in Jerusalem
he tells us as he spreads his arms
wide in passion.

I am reminded of
the flash of police lights trapped
in the mirror of still-wet paint,
you and I running
beneath the overpass
into the thick woods to hide
from God getting out of his patrol car.

I can't remember what
we were trying to say
to the rest of the world.

I can only hope that
it mattered more than the mere
rebellious "I"
only hope it had matter enough

to justify daring each other to
the wrong side
of the rules we had memorized
in Catechism.

Only hope that the slick of paint
got us arrested for believing
in something about art
something weighty about the world.

Muddy World

*Honor requires that he die without confession. That he
die uttering a word of honor in the face of his captors and
torturers. Honor requires that he proclaim his community
with those with whom no one has anything in common.*

—Alphonso Lingis,
The Community of Those Who Have Nothing in Common

The Tonlé Sap got me there in 2006,
part muddy river, part lake,
from Phnom Penh to Angkor Wat,
the same as my own Mississippi.
If I paddle against the stream,
New Orleans runs into St. Louis.
I compare the navigable miles:
2,161 to something much less.

In 2013 I still read the 1976
University Society Encyclopedia,
to gather facts around me like the
photos of daughters, nephews,
nieces, friends whose names I fear
I'll lose in another 15 years unless
I keep them pasted to my refrigerator
door, reading the collage on weekends.

These 20 hardback volumes of blue,
the front cover embossed with
a small gold circle of earth,
the flattened continent I live on
south of an empty Arctic center,
the land of Kampuchea oddly north,
as if it truly were north of Asian tundra.

I remember how my husband and I
purchased the hefty books,
anticipating a family to educate
into the history of people far away,
but having no funds for annual updates,
not knowing what was happening
on the other side of the world
even as the entry on Cambodia ended:
"Phnom-Penh fell to the rebels on
April 16, 1975. An estimated two
million people were then herded
from the capital and other cities
by the victors and set to 'till the fields.'"

When I walked across the killing fields
of Choeung Ek, I remembered being 8,
walking through the cemetery where
we had just buried one of my cousins,
my father maneuvering me between
the graves: "Never walk on the dead."
But how could I avoid stepping on them,
with pits and paths so arbitrary
and no headstones to guide me.

In 2005 there was no navigating
among the photos at Tuol Sleng,
hundreds of faces on stiff boards,
in tight rows and columns,
hundreds of people with names
once upon a time, me recording
those that had been translated
for people who pronounce my
language—Mong Sam Oeun,
Uy Ren—clumps of letters,
sounds I stumble over.

But then a woman whose name
was stamped only in Khmer,
followed by the number 462.
She held a baby, sleeping
or something much less.
It was in the woman's eyes
that I read the exact distance
between her home planet
and the muddy world I live on.

Wedged Words

Poets love from afar,
wedging word into word
to safeguard all they love,

a buffer made of the crackling
pain of an ice-stormed tree
and the wretched ecstasy

of watching its glass-burdened
limbs bend to near-breaking
freedom, a refusal to name

the terror of crashing, swathing
it in such florid phrases as
"love breaking into grief,"

this buffer of spoken air
huffing between sky
and the finality of something

we've given so much thought
to euphemizing but never
daring to say simply.

Unashamed Season

This is why I write so abstractly,
our violent mother having cleared
a path for our brother to follow,
doing what no man should do
to his sisters,
                    to be carried away from there
                    and all its grief
to prepare me to take myself back,
ready for that throat-closing stone
of the past,
ready for this time of clothing
old-story bones.

This is why I carry you on my back
to and then up the sycamore that stands
watch over my new neighborhood
as I tell our old story,
the sycamore's hide looking as if
it had been stripped bare of bark,
stripped down to bone
and shining with sun-reflecting light,
                    this unhesitant nakedness necessary
                    for seeing
full-bore.

This is why it must be winter
for speaking true to you about us,
peeled of all the brighter shades of green,
leaving me with just a few words
leftover from the scraps of childhood,
                    but none of that purple bruise
                    and scar talk
to describe the color and texture
of our story.

This is why I sit with you in silence
for one last moment at the topmost
spread of the sycamore,

        one last time to breathe in innocence
        through naked unashamed branches

that nod graciously
to the nearby spruce still bound
to its own sharp needles,
holding them tight through every season,
even summer,
as if to say
it still can't bear to have anyone
climbing around in the heart of it,
the heart of us.

Spontaneous Human Combustion

Spontaneous human combustion is possible
where bone strikes bone, a pestle in a mortar,
and I wish I weren't speaking figuratively here.

The cactus of the Atacama Desert of Chile can
dance beyond its demise, a rain stick shivering
into smoke simply by being flipped over and over.

But might the slow friction, the interior rub
of a chant dance ritual, also accelerate
the conflagration of tribe clan family?

I study the end of cultures, the drama
of the resolute dance of tradition, knowing
sometimes a death march looks like ballet.

But more often a day-to-day domino effect,
like my own family tipped over and over,
the cliché of bodies soaked in cheap gin.

Here is the ritual of fire: a book of matches
near the bottle my brother trembles to his mouth
twenty thirty times a day in his easy chair.

In an overstuffed chair the sudden blaze
always shocks, shivers into disbelief,
the body bewildered by its own detonation.

In dreams I see the stick in my own hand
but I am deaf to its rattle, deaf to the *requiem
aeternam* hovering above the fire's embers.

The Present

Oh, my loves,
do not peer too deeply into the beyond
not the above you
not the beneath you
not the behind you
not the reaches of the far far before you
(yes, I mean both kinds of be-fore)

Keep your attention on the literal
pattern of the trees in your front
(and side and back) yards
as they glitter with light
on the leaves of summer's fecundity
on the ice that clings to winter's woes
(yes, even such sad images will sustain)

Press your palms to the bark
every day
to feel the roughness of what matters
after every thought and theory
(every how and why of the past and future)
have had their way with you

To feel what we still (and ever) call
real (no matter what trick of our minds
that might be)
to feel what it means to be
endeared
to the enduring presence

Tree

I see you
                watching
over
all the earth

I know you
wait
                noticing
                everything
even me

As I step
                closer
the skin
of your limbs
                ripples

I move
                closer still
my arms
cooled
by your shadow

I feel
your shadow
                anticipating

I am not
imagining
                this
invitation

Your rough bark
body
                welcoming
my arms

Your shadow
                mine

To the Untethered Word

You, who whirl
through the Fates, scattering them.
You, my tornado.

I watch you spin past.
You, stirring the tide.
You, circumventing magic.

You, flipping off the ineffable.
You who are your own marvel,
how does your body stand it?

What do you do with all that
sunshine, all that light
glaring at mystery?

Do you miss shadows?
Do you miss depth perception?
The taste of human salt?

Something Crackles Here

Some thing here inside,
at the side of this poem, near the straight edge,
just inside the stiff branches that the lines make
at the trunk of the left margin, not extending as far
                                        as the right jagged edge,
only as far as our eyes can take in,
only this far
down
the branch,
this line crackling with ice,
and this line
and this one,
can you hear it?

I want you to be able to hear
everything it says, every thing the ice declares
about itself, every single thing the world says
when it wakes up here on the edge of us.

Are you prepared for the sound of it, for our next line,
perhaps the rush of birds, the swoosh of them just before dawn,
the shock of them to flip you awake,
to flip you from the hammock you are used to dreaming in,
to flip you into their chattering world?

There's that crackling again.
Can you hear the ice melting just outside,
here
just past my window,
there
on branches in ever-so-still air,
something like the rustle of your stiff silk dress
against the bark of the oak tree as you were inviting
my kiss, but the crinkle of it just a bit higher pitched?

I want this old-style pitching woo to matter to you,
want you
to shiver to the edge of our planet,
or if not that
then I hope you remember how to listen to the world
of your own making, ready for the whoosh of it
waking you up on the leafy bed of your own choosing.

At least that . . .
that . . . if you're not able to travel past the edge of this
                                        forest of wordy lines,
if not able
to lie in my bed and listen
here
for the murmur of each day's dawn,
if not able to bear the weight
of ice on the old oak tree scraping my window.

Note from My Alter Ego

Why such resistance to me,
to my mixed metaphors, this leap
across a mere arroyo-sized chasm?

Your poetry is stiff as concrete,
near-impervious to the sogging
rain I'd have melt your skin,

hard as the darkest chocolate
unyielding in a warm mouth.
How I desire you to clamber

out of your shadow box of nouns,
to bold forth into purple sorcery,
to materialize next to me,

or at least to conjure and toss
a new word into this verbatorium.
Sex yourself with a verb of me.

Fearing the Middle

How I keep starting over
at the treetop
wobbling off its highest
limb
as if only my dive through air
mattered
as if I never crawled up into
heartwood
never got up after the fall
never
found a nest among ripened
milkweed
pods spitting feather-tailed
seeds

How I am obsessed with
the question
of whether I jumped or fell
from the elm

How I keep holding my breath
through
the first sentence of the story
though
I know the oxygen I take in
won't stay
oxygen long enough to span
the middle

How I pin all my breath on
beginnings
ever fearing the middle of all
stories
or the moment the sentence
ends

Shadow's Low Drama

You are shadow, always in between
matter and light as you coil into
a hiss, coil then drop from the elm,
flattened by some internal mystery,
the logic of you compressing
the space between thick and thin,
sphere and plane.

I would have you be pure light
burning my eye's curved surface,
flashing into cavities, this an act
of high drama.

Though blinded in the process,
I'd still prefer that kind of poison,
that dense and shadowless fang,
white as bone.

But my soul sits in the rough elm
as easily as on a silky bleached
mud plain.

I belong to shadow, to that side
of lovers and mothers, to that
list of nouns and verbs never
scripted into three-dimensional
space but ironed flat to suit this
sheet of paper, itself only seeming
the color of light, its true nature
a cipher that goes by the name
White.

What kind of a word is it
whose name belies the power
of shadow at the very heart
of light, its horizonless source
beneath the edge of this page,
its underside.

Here at the sidewalk's edge,
its apparent end, I may turn
and begin again, startled again
by the hiss of my shadow, you,
thickening again into drama,
the low drama of our second act
where one of us takes the blade
in the gut, the other bleeds out
revenge, both of us flattened
into remorse.

It's all the same, whichever of us
drops into despair of the other
for in the middle of the third act
we will come round to sense,
my deflated body, my soul,
needing shadow, you, to smudge
texture upon my forehead,
you to dust me with fingerprints.

Practicing The Otherwhere of Mud

I prefer clean-sliced words,
neat rows of verbs
arranging nouns around
themselves just so.

But I like to imagine myself intoxicated
by pebbles mixed with muddy-world sound,
each abrading the other, an excess of nouns and
adjectives and adverbs sloppily crawling all over
the insides of verbs
and pulling their stuffing out, the way your cat breaks
the weave on your dark brown chair and
pulls
the unbleached cotton through in not-so-delicate
clumps.

From across the room the curls of cotton look exactly like
a nest of maggots, just-hatched
larvae ready
to crawl down the arms, down legs,
to the floor, intent on making it all the way across
the ocean of oak flooring to chew
on my toes
on the other side of meaning.

Right now I am forcing myself to leave the odd phrasing
above—I have no idea what it means—and, yes,
willing myself to accept
the anthropomorphic intentionality of fly larvae,
even to go so far as to let them live freely
freely on this crumpled page, for how can
I break

into texture the way I break
into song, freely
without care for where
songs erupt,
unless I practice
practice
moving verbs in, moving verbs
among, moving
verbs into all the tidy corners,
verbs the otherwhere of mud.

Haiku Against Word Puzzles

Topsy-turvy words,
I flip them around, trying
to own every pause

Pausing to catch all
but not reaching the last word,
trapped in the middle

The middle being
Shadow itself spreading me
across timelessness

Shadow's timelessness
moving like the Möbius,
nothing segmented

Unsegmented time,
all one washed-clean gradience,
all one utterance

I, one utterance,
till the light overtakes me,
pleats me into time

Pleats of opposites,
mere sequences, day and dark,
words belying sense

Sense flipped past meaning,
overwriting timelessness,
displacing Shadow

Shadow's replacement
flattened here in this puzzle,
all these ill-fit words

How to Begin the Day

There is a choice here.
Better to choose the shadow.
See the interplay

between us and light.
Shadow pacing the distance,
a sure-footed guide.

Better yet, simply
close our eyes. Listen as birds
chirp into being.

Best of all, leave them
open as we warble, spell-
casting the sun. Rise.

Letting the Magic Show

Shadows protect you and me
even as we sometimes misuse their power to hide
ourselves away from the world,
inside our own pallid skin.

I can laugh with you as you tell
the overwritten story of your life,
a melodrama—mine too, mine too—of dastardly men
you've managed to escape,
or almost, after years of therapy.
We both know every good story has its antagonist.

You've read my memoir of the Mommy Dearest who
turned herself inside out
for love of her children,
her fierce love saving us—well most of us—and I hope
saving herself from the hellfire
she feared would be her end.
And you didn't flinch.

I've read your horror tales of the psychopathic woman
who decapitates children
and mummifies their heads to keep as trophies.
She makes sure to feed them well,
even in the winter, for muscle and bone need
iron and calcium all year long,
the brain of each and every child needs the protein
that binds love to dendrites.

I ask you to open the cabinet
where she keeps the plump faces of babies.
You ask me what kind of meat

goes into the stew that makes my writing so famous.
We laugh and laugh at the thought
of you and me unzipping our skins to enter the story,
to try wickedness on for size,
knowing we never could,
neither of us having such power
in any such shadowland.

We do not talk of what
blood—whose blood—we might wish to shed,
instead telling each other fairy tales
of wicked witches transformed into thorny
woods that any fool knows never to enter.

But we do, we do—it's our destiny,
our vocation—to find irony buried there,
fertilizing the undergrowth.

We know who our shadows are.
We know the branches of the witch-wood
are our own spreading hands, ours the sap
dripping from thorny limbs,
our odor rising from the ground, filling the air
with possibility.

I ignore your scarlet wrist scars
as you bare your limbs so delicately cut.
I admire the tattoos slithering up your arms
and wait—I have learned to be patient, not to force
revelation's power—for the next
story you might need to tell,
for the magic show of ink on your glowing skin.

Sea Foam

Each wave rocks up and up
like a child on a swing
expecting at the next lift to fly.

Water's simple melody

                rocking

between two notes
as if a bird announcing itself
a bird calling to bird
its slightly older twin
then a third note invited in
the trio playing an arpeggio

                together

before they quarrel

                before

they burst and foam

                apart.

Only now do I let myself enter
the frame   sitting
here in the damp sand
with my camera's eye

                watching

the rising pitch and tumble

                watching

each resurrected wave
collide with the shore
collide and vanish

                gone

just like that
like the camera's aperture
released into light
and just as suddenly
closed

                              emptied
senseless.

                              Before
I can join the roiling melody
just before   now   now   now
please   let me
put my camera down
set my eyes aside and   foam
into the pitch and yaw of song.

A Reply to Lake Erie

Lake Erie crashes today, as if to say "Rain? Wind?
You call this stormy weather? I'll show you a storm.
I am the storm.   I, Tempest."

Here comes the drip of you
and more of you to dribble
                           to run now
                           to crash into
me, words   that can never contain you
                           never encompass you
not even the metaphors of you.

You flood across any words that might
parse   you
into manageable segments.

You overwhelm the page.

You bleach the ink.

You wash the paper fibers down
to the pulp
                           that in its youth was dried
into flat sheets
                           that would love to ripple
in the wind
                           that would wave gladly
reminding me of the expanse of wheat
fields now floating in my waterlogged
memory   so limited
                           so sectioned off
                           so measured out
across their windy shadowland.

This page and the runes of me upon it
unprepared   for the massive splash
                          thrown up
by the horizonless lake before me,
                    by you.

Me   as vulnerable
as this soaked journal on someone's lap
                          as artless
as heat-bleached wheat
heads bowing and stooping before
a driving rain.
                    So biblical.

So overpowering that the sound
of any words
                    I might conjure up
to match the fury,
                    your fury,
becomes as nothing.

All this nothing compared to you,
                    Tempest.

And yet I must try.
                    I, Drowning Words.

The Found Object Imagines a Life

Lying here on the sidewalk
I will wait for someone
like you
to stop.

Pick me up.

Something round-edged
soft in the middle
an invitation to press
your index finger
into me.

Just so.

I'll give under your touch
seduce you with warmth
the way the spring sun feels
on your exposed arms
your throat
your lips
your eyelids
as you step into the street
of cars.

Enthralled.

I won't release you
no found object ever does
even though I'll feel
sympathy
for the inconvenience I cause
your collapsed lung
your cracked femur.

You'll live.

You'll spend
the rest of your life
confounded yet fascinated
by the persistence
of me.

My promise beckoning
or is it my premise.

Do I remind you
of something you read
or something you heard
that catchy tune
that hum in your head
that multisyllabic mantra
not to be shaken off.

Your own private earwig.

I'll dangle
from the edge of you
coercing you to compose
poems about me
to recite me over and over.

An ineffectual exorcism.

When you die
I'll be the crawling script
just under the parchment
of your skin
to be read from the inside
out.

Read me one last time.

Only at the funeral
will I ooze through
the seams of you
me releasing you
as they close the lid.

Me escaping your life
to make promises elsewhere.

Acknowledgments

Many thanks to Dr. Ross Tangedal, Director of Cornerstone Press, Editorial Director Grace Dahl, and Production Director Amanda Leibham for their guidance through the publication process. They not only provided publishing expertise but, also, patience with one who sometimes can't think beyond the shape of a poem. Ross, this book would not exist without your encouragement.

Many of the poems of this book would still be rough drafts without the support and thoughtful critiques of members of my SwampFire community of writers and artists. Thank you to Amy Drees, Bex Miller, Eva English, Jan Maher, Jerri Courtney, Joyce Meier, Marcy Bauman, Marian Plant, and Rachel Baker for all those insightful discussions over tea and around the campfire.

A special thank you to Steve Smith and Jan Bechtel, artists—friends—who helped me find words for my visual and tactile experiences, who helped me give voice to the "found objects" that surround me.

And to the founder of SwampFire, Dawn Burns, I cannot say thank you enough for your friendship. For your patience with rough drafts of poems. For sharing your wonderful imagination on long, lovely road trips. And for building the community of writers that continues to support me and so many others.

To the editors of the journals, collections, and chapbook where the following poems appeared, thank you for all you do to bring poetry into our lives.

"The Art of Love" and "The Fall" in *Sheila-Na-Gig*

"Blue Spruce" in *Kansas City Voices*

"Eclipse of the Past" in *Sky Island Journal*

"Feuding Clans" in *The Comstock Review*

"Planet of Chairs" in *Cold Mountain Review*

"Sgraffito" in *Print-Oriented Bastards*

"Sonic Booms" and "Things That Bite or Drag You Underground" in *South Florida Poetry Journal* (*SoFloPoJo*)

"What Shoes Do" in *South 85 Journal*

"What Hands Ask of Stone" and "Persephone in Summer" in *The Offbeat*

"Eleusinian Mystery," "Diving In," and "Four Words of the Apocalypse" in *The Spectacle*

"Ts'its'tsi'nako," "Reading Tarot," "Tiresias Among the Sycamores," and "The Spider Talks to Her Creation" in the chapbook, *Some Gods Don't Need Saints* (Finishing Line Press 2016)

"Thirteen Versions of the Big Bang" in *No Contact*

"Job, Fresh from Apotheosis," "Embroidery," "Sin of the Cyborg," and "Miriam, Bitter Sea" in the "Digital Eves: Transgression/Transcendence in Cyberspace" collection of *WomenWriters.net*

"Potter's Retreat, Poet's Ground" and "*Nox*, Rain" in *SwampFire.org*

"A Murder of Crows" and "On Seeing, Too Close" in *SLAB* (*Sound & Literary Art Book*)

"A Map to Live On" in *Wild Roof Journal*

"Marble Love" in *Abyss & Apex*

"To Invent What We Desire" in *Third Wednesday*

"How to Begin the Day" in *Closed Eye Open*

"Muddy World" and "Imagining Life as a Graffiti Artist" in *MidAmerica*

Mary Catherine Harper, a 2018 Ohio Arts Council Individual Excellence Award winner, was selected as the 2019 Ohio Arts Council Poetry Resident at the Fine Arts Work Center of Cape Cod. She has made her home at the confluence of the Auglaize and Maumee rivers in Ohio and organizes the yearly SwampFire Retreat for artists and writers at 4 Corners Gallery in Angola, Indiana.

She is a two-time winner of the Gwendolyn Brooks Poetry Prize, for "Muddy World" and "Imagining Life as a Graffiti Artist," and her poetry has appeared in numerous journals, including *The Comstock Review*, *Cold Mountain Review*, *Pudding Magazine*, *New England Review*, *SLAB*, *MidAmerica*, *Tanka Journal*, *The Spectacle*, *Print-Oriented Bastards*, *Sheila-Na-Gig*, and *The Offbeat*. Her chapbook, *Some Gods Don't Need Saints*, was published in 2016. See marycatherineharper.org for more information.

www.ingramcontent.com/pod-product-compliance
Lightning Source LLC
Chambersburg PA
CBHW020252130626
46549CB00005B/2186